The people of the world made God sad because they did bad things and hurt each other.

But God found one good and obedient man named Noah. "I will send a flood, but I will save your family and the animals," God said.

Many people laughed at Noah. "You are crazy!" they said. "It's never even rained before. Ha! Ha! Ha! Ho! Ho! Ho!"

But Noah didn't stop just because people made fun of him. He kept on working and building the boat. What a big job it was!

When Noah finally finished building the big Ark, God sent two of each kind of animal. They all went into the boat. There were big animals and little ones, fast animals and slow ones too.

Noah's family and the animals were now safe and sound inside.

It rained for so many many days. The boat rocked and splashed around. The animals inside felt like thy were on a roller-coaster ride, while the fish outside had more water than ever to swim in.

Some time later, Noah sent a bird, to fly up high and down low, and to check out the situation of the ground.

It finally came back with a branch. "That means dry land is nearby!" said Noah joyfully.

They breathed fresh air and stepped on the ground! It felt wonderful not to be rocking on a boat any more.

Noah praised God for His greatness and for keeping them safe! God put the very first rainbow in the sky. "Now every time you see one, remember My love and power!" God said.

Noah continued to love and trust God thoughout the rest of his life. What a great lesson we can learn from him.

www.ingramcontent.com/pod-product-compliance
Lightning Source LLC
Chambersburg PA
CBHW040007080526
44586CB00027B/2913